BEST 25 PLACES TO VISIT IN
ROME

Don't forget to get your FREE book below.

https://bit.ly/25PlacesParis

1. Colosseum

The Colosseum, a large amphitheatre that once held 65,000 spectators, is Rome's number one attraction. Gladiators fought each other as well as wild animals in the arena of the Colosseum. The Colosseum's massive 'ruins' include the stands, arena, and underground spaces of the largest Roman amphitheatre. Because of the high volume of visitors, it is strongly advised to purchase tickets to the Colosseum in advance, which is regarded as one of the world's seven modern wonders. More information on the well-known landmark 'Colosseum.'

Taking a guided tour is the best way to avoid long lines and get to know the famous monument in depth. This one skips the lines and takes you to the Colosseum, Roman Forum, and Palatine Hill with an expert local guide.

To avoid long lines that can last several hours, it is best to arrive early in the morning or buy an entrance ticket on the Palatine Hill, where there are usually fewer people and the cost of admission is combined.

Memories

Date:

2. Trevi Fountain of Rome

  The Trevi Fountain, also known as the 'Fontana di Trevi,' is perhaps the most renowned fountain in the world, and certainly in Rome. Bernini originally created the baroque fountain in the Piazza di Trevi square for Pope Clemens XII. However, it was not completed until 50 years later, after Nicola Salvi's (less expensive) remodeling. From 1732 to 1762, the building was under construction. Many films featuring the Trevi Fountain, including as La Dolce Vita, Angels and Demons, The Lizzie McGuire Movie, and Roman Holiday, have contributed to the fountain's reputation.

  The Trevi Fountain, which stands about 30 meters tall, was built against the Palazzo Poli building's back wall. The figure of the maritime god Neptune, dragged to the sea on his shell-shaped chariot by two winged horses and tritons, stands in the center beneath the arch (young gods of the sea). One horse is quiet and obedient, while the other is rambunctious. They represent the sea's changing tides. The two statues in the niches next to Neptune (crafted by Filippo della Valle) symbolize Abundance on the left and Health on the right. The name 'La Fontana di Trevi' comes from the words tre via, which means three highways. At the fountain's location, three roadways used to meet.

Memories

Date:

3. The Pantheon Rome

The Pantheon is one of the most well-preserved Roman structures. The Pantheon was handed to the Pope by Emperor Hadrian in 608. It is unclear what purpose the edifice served in those days. The modern cathedral has a wonderfully big and open dome, as well as some remarkable funeral monuments (painter Raphael and a few Italian rulers) (oculus). You can visit the Pantheon for free during your city vacation in Rome.

Rome's Pantheon is a real architectural marvel. To visit it today is to be transported back to the Roman Empire itself, as it is known as the "sphinx of the Campus Martius," referring to the enigmas provided by its look and history, as well as the site in Rome where it was created. The Roman Pantheon is unlikely to appear on most people's shortlists of architectural symbols, but it should: it is one of the most copied structures in history.

Memories

Date:

4. St. Peter's Basilica

 The Basilica of St. Peter in Vaticano, also known as the 'Basilica di San Pietro in Vaticano,' is the spiritual heart of the Catholic Church and the papal palace. The massive basilica, which stands close to St Peter's Square in the sovereign state of Vatican City, was built on what is thought to be Peter's grave. The crypts of St. Peter's Basilica contain 148 papal graves, as well as treasures such as Bernini's baldachin and Michelangelo's 'La Pieta.' Plan ahead of time if you want to visit St Peter's, otherwise you'll be standing in line for a long time.

 The structure, known as the Popes' Church, is a popular pilgrimage destination. The basilica and its nearby St. Peter's Square, which frequently gather tens of thousands of Catholics, are utilized for a number of liturgies presided over by the pope throughout the year. St. Peter's Basilica is one of only four great basilicas in the world, along with the Basilica of St. John Lateran (San Giovanni in Laterano), the Basilica of Santa Maria Maggiore, and the Basilica of St. Paul Outside the Walls (all three of which are in Rome). St. Peter's was the greatest church in Christendom until 1989. At that year, the freshly constructed basilica in Yamoussoukro, Côte d'Ivoire, surpassed it in size.

Memories

Date:

5. Vatican Museums & Sistine Chapel

   The popes built a huge art collection over the years, ranging from Roman items and religious relics to countless paintings. The Vatican Museums have 54 ornately furnished rooms where visitors may see the Catholic church's art treasures. The iconic Sistine Chapel is likely to be the highlight for many tourists. The church, which features beautiful Michelangelo frescoes, is most renowned for hosting the conclave when a new Pope is elected. This attraction has by far the longest lineups due to the large number of visitors. If you don't want to wait in the blazing sun for more than two hours, skip-the-line tickets are a must.

Memories

Date:

6. Roman sights of Forum Romanum & Palatine

　A stroll through the Roman Forum provides insight into the formation of the ancient Roman Empire.
　The Romans drained marshland and transformed it into a political and social hub. The Forum was Rome's marketplace, as well as a gathering place for triumphal processions, criminal prosecutions, and gladiatorial contests.
　The Roman Forum formerly housed some of the city's oldest and most important structures; today, it's a jumble of ruins, including shrines and temples like the House of the Vestal Virgins. The oldest monuments in the Roman Forum date from the sixth century BC and are from Rome's earliest kings.
　The Forum was eventually abandoned in the Middle Ages and gradually buried beneath layers of earth. Some temples were converted into churches, allowing them to be preserved over time.
　The Forum Romanum was exploited as a marble and stone quarry during the Renaissance. However, it wasn't until 1898 that excavations began, uncovering the site we see today.

Memories

Date:

7. Piazza Navona

The Piazza Navona is one of Rome's most beautiful squares. The square's elongated design stems from its historical use as a Roman athletics stadium. A variety of fountains, including Bernini's 'La Fontana dei Quattro Fiumi,' an attractive obelisk, and the excavations of Domitianus' former stadium are among the attractions on the area. Piazza Navona is also a bustling square with a variety of street performers, cafés, and terraces.

 The Piazza Navona is one of Rome's most beautiful and well-known squares. Emperor Domitian commissioned this square, which has an unusual, elongated design, in 86 CE. Its initial role as a stadium for athletics tournaments (Circus Agonalis) with seating for 20,000 people gave it this shape. During the sweltering summer months, Pope Innocent even organized so-called "water sports," in which the entire square was submerged. Houses were built where the stands used to be after the Roman Empire fell apart, but the vast sports field remained undeveloped and would later become Piazza Navona.

Memories

Date:

8. Spanish Steps (Piazza di Spagna)

The Piazza di Spagna (English: Square of Spain) is a well-known square in Rome. The name stems from the Palazzo di Spagna, which has been the seat of the Spanish Embassy for the Vatican since the sixteenth century and is located on this plaza.

The Piazza di Spagna is located in one of Rome's most attractive areas, among the high streets Via dei Condotti, Via Frattina, and Via del Babuino, which are home to a number of remarkable seventeenth and eighteenth-century villas.

Piazza del Popolo is reached by walking down Via del Babuino. The Flaminio Obelisk, one of Rome's tallest obelisks, was housed in the Circus Maximus and stands in the square's center.

Climb the steps from Piazza del Popolo to the summit of Pincian Hill for some of the best views of Rome.

Memories

Date:

9. Galleria & Villa Borghese

   The largest and most beautiful park in Rome is known as Villa Borghese. This estate was built around the villa of the same name and once belonged to the very wealthy cardinal Scipione Borghese. It has been in the hands of the Rome municipality since 1903 and functions as a public park. The 'Galleria Borghese,' a museum presenting Borghese's extensive private art collection, is also located in the park. Sculptures and paintings by Caravaggio, Rubens, Bernini, and Leonardo da Vinci may be found in the gallery.

Memories

Date:

10. Basilica di Santa Maria Maggiore

   The largest ('Maggiore') of Rome's eighty Mary churches is the 'Basilica Papale di Santa Maria Maggiore.' On the direction of Pope Sixtus III, this church was built on Esquiline Hill in 432 and is one of Rome's seven pilgrim churches and four papal basilicas (the others being St. Peter's Basilica, San Giovanni in Laterano, and San Paolo Fuori Le Mura). The Basilica of Santa Maria Maggiore was built on the spot where Pope Liberius saw the Virgin Mary in a dream. On the 5th of August, in the middle of summer, a layer of snow fell on the hill. Every year, white flower petals are dropped from the ceiling to honor this day.

   Many of the mosaics in the basilica (in the nave and on the arch, for example) are unique to the structure. The basilica's huge marble columns are considerably older, having come from an ancient Roman structure. The golden, coffered ceiling, commissioned by the controversial Pope Alexander VI and created with the first gold Columbus brought back from America, is unique in this church.

Memories

Date:

11. Sights of Trastevere

    The charming neighborhood Trastevere is located on the opposite bank of the Tiber River, south of the Vatican. The name Trastevere comes from the Latin trans Tiberium, which means "beyond the Tiber." This historic working-class neighborhood, with its tiny lanes and medieval houses, comes alive at night with restaurants, trattorias, and pizzerias, owing to the influx of tourists. Take a stroll through this authentically Italian Rome neighborhood or unwind on one of the many café terraces.

    Trastevere has been one of the city's 14 districts since the days of Emperor Augustus, and it was also walled. Julius Caesar was one of several notable Romans who erected villas in this area. The neighborhood's lovely atmosphere dates back to medieval times, with its maze of many narrow and twisting alleyways.

Memories

Date:

12. Castel Sant'Angelo

Emperor Hadrian ordered the construction of the Castel Sant'Angelo as a mausoleum in the second century. Until 590, when Pope Gregory I witnessed archangel Michael sheathing his sword on top of the mausoleum during a plague to announce the end of the pandemic, the mausoleum was not identified with the name of archangel Michael. Later, Pope Pius II built a chapel near the alleged appearance of the archangel. Peter Anton von Verschaffelt sculpted the magnificent bronze statue of Archangel Michael in 1753. The film adaptation of Dan Brown's Angels & Demons made the Castle of the Holy Angel in Rome famous, with the castle serving as a hideout for the Illuminati.

Memories

Date:

13. Vittorio Emanuele II Monument

 The monument honoring the first Italian king Vittorio Emanuelle II, which is located next to the Piazza Venezia plaza, is one of Rome's most notable structures. The structure is also known as the 'Altara della Patria,' or 'Altar of the Fatherland,' and it symbolizes Italy's unification. It is also known by nicknames such as 'typewriter' and 'wedding cake' among Romans. The massive white structure also houses a museum and the unknown soldier's tomb, which is guarded by two soldiers.

Memories

Date:

14. Arcibasilica di San Giovanni in Laterano

The 'Arcibasilica di San Giovanni in Laterano,' or Archbasilica of St. John Lateran in Rome, was established in 313 by Emperor Constantine the Great. Emperor Constantine was the emperor who, in 313, granted freedom of religion to the Roman empire, including Christianity, with the 'Edict of Milan.' The church was once a papal residence. After the papal return from Avignon (1309-1377), it lost this function, owing to a series of fires. The cathedral, along with St. Peter's Basilica, remained one of Rome's four papal churches (the other two Papal churches are Santa Maria Maggiore and San Paolo Fuori le Mura).

It's worth noting that this church serves as the cathedral for the diocese of Rome, making it the city's most prominent church.

Memories

Date:

15. Piazza del Popolo

  Piazza del Popolo is a monumental and magnificent square at the top of Via del Babuino, Via di Ripetta, and Via del Corso, the three principal avenues of Rome's old center.

The area's urbanization began in the second half of the 16th century, with the construction of the Fontana del Trullo, designed by Giacomo Della Porta and now located in Piazza Nicosia, and the subsequent positioning of the Flaminio obelisk, which stands about 24 meters tall and was moved from the Circus Maximus by order of Sixtus V in 1589; it was the first obelisk to be moved to Rome, at the time of Augustus,
  Pope Pius IV commissioned Michelangelo to design the exterior façade of today's Porta del Popolo (the ancient Porta Flaminia). However, the artist delegated the work to Nanni di Baccio Bigio, who completed it between 1562 and 1565. The statement etched on the inside façade, sculpted by Bernini for Alexander VII on the occasion of Christina of Sweden's entry in Rome in 1655, is "Felici faustoque ingressui MDCLV" (For a joyous and auspicious entrance).

Memories

Date:

16. Via Appia Antica & Catacombs

   The Appian Way, also known as the Via Appia Antica, is one of Rome's oldest roadways and once functioned as a major entrance route into the city. The route once extended all the way to Brundisium, which is now Brindisi in the heel of Italy. The consul Appius Claudius Caecus, who commissioned the road's construction in 312 BCE, was given the name. The main purpose at the time was to transfer troops more rapidly during the Second Samnite War, but it was also to make day-to-day goods delivery between Rome and Campania easier.

   The paved stone road is known as the "regina viarium," which means "queen of the roads." This is due to the road's importance, as well as the beauty of the terrain the Via Appia passes through. Part of the road (beginning at the Cecelia Metella funerary monument) still retains antique paving stones that reveal the wear of the carriage tracks. The verdant cypresses and several ruins that flank the cobblestone path give the Via Appia Antica a lovely aura.

Memories

Date:

17. Domus Aurea

Emperor Nero had the massive palace complex Domus Aurea ("Golden House") erected in Rome after a severe fire in 64 AD. According to legend, Nero ignited the fire personally in order to make room for his castle. With abundance of marble, ivory, and gold leaf walls, the 80-hectare structure with more than 150 rooms was Rome's most stunning and opulent palace. The palace had an outstanding entrance with a colonnade and a 35-meter-high statue of Nero himself at the time, which could be seen from the Roman Forum.

Only small parties with a guide are permitted to see Domus Aurea. The best part about this trip is that you get to view what Nero's palace looked like in the past thanks to virtual reality glasses. Because much work is being done on the restoration of Domus Aurea during the week, the tour is only available on weekends.

Memories

Date:

18. Domus Romane

Palazzo Valentini, built in the 16th century, has served a variety of purposes and is named after banker and consul general Vincenzo Valentini, who purchased the property in 1827. Since 1873, the palace has served as the capital of the province of Rome. This, however, is hardly a compelling incentive to pay a visit to the property. The reason for your visit is a hidden gem discovered by chance seven meters beneath the Palazzo Valentini in 2005: nearly 1900 m2 of well-preserved remains of a former Roman private bath house and two residences ("Domus Romane") of powerful families from the imperial era, which were beautifully decorated with mosaics, marble, and wall decorations.

The site is now exposed to the public in a unique fashion, following years of restoration by art historians and archaeologists. Not only can you see the complex's ruins through a glass floor, but you can also take an augmented reality tour of the digs, which includes computer animations and virtual reconstructions. You will spend an hour and a half on a virtual tour of the apartments, walls, and baths, imagining yourself in ancient Rome. At the conclusion of the Domus Romane trip, you will learn more about Trajan's Column, which is located just across from the Palazzo Valentini and provides a great photo opportunity.

Memories

Date:

19. Palazzo Colonna or Palazzo Doria Pamphilj

A number of spectacular city palaces from the 16th and 17th century may be seen in Rome. These mansions are opulent, having private collections of paintings and frescoes that are vast. At least one palace and its associated galleries should be visited during your city stay. I favor two palaces: the Colonna Gallery, which I recommend if you are in Rome on a Saturday morning, and the Doria Pamphilj Gallery, which you may visit on other days.

The Palazzo Colonna is one of Rome's oldest and largest private residences, and a hidden gem that you should not miss on a Saturday morning in Rome. The Colonna dynasty began construction on the palace in the 14th century. The palace's facade is Renaissance-style, and you won't see it in the street setting.

The Galleria Doria Pamphilj is a museum housed in the Doria family's 16th century mansion (Palazzo Doria Pamphilj), which houses mostly paintings from the family's private collection. The paintings are displayed in eleven stunning locations, including the throne room and ballroom. This is a fantastic site to visit in Rome, partly because it has yet to be discovered by mainstream tourism.

Memories

Date:

20. Basilica di San Clemente al Laterano

At first appearance, the basilica consecrated to Pope Clement I does not appear to be one of Rome's most spectacular cathedrals. Multiple church buildings were built on top of one other over the years, making this Basilica of San Clemente unique. During your visit, you will be able to learn about the church's history through excavations of a 4th-century church, a 1st-century secret church, and Roman foundations.

Memories

Date:

21. Capuchin crypt

The Capuchin crypt is a particularly special, but also scary, spot in Rome. In 1525, the Capuchins split from the Franciscans in order to live more authentically in the spirit of Saint Francis and return to the basics. They wore sandals without socks and a hooded tunic to keep their heads warm. The capuchins get their name from this cap

The museum of the Capuchins' crypt is the first stop on your tour. More information on the Capuchins' history and the crypts can be found here. A painting by Caravaggio depicting Saint Francis can be found in this museum. Then you'll go to the crypt, which has five chapels with bones, skulls, and occasionally even whole skeletons, as well as one boneless chapel with the altar that is moderately illuminated. 'Quello che voi siete noi eravamo, quello che noi siamo voi sarete' (English "Exactly what you are now, we once were, what we are now will become you") concludes the journey in the final chapel.Following that, you can go to the connected church, 'Santa Maria della Concezione dei Cappuccini.'.

Memories

Date:

22. Four papal basilicas

The papal basilicas are Rome's four most important churches. Each of these patriarchal basilicas has its own 'Holy Door.' During the so-called jubilee, these Holy Doors are opened once every 25 years. During a jubilee, the faithful can gain an indulgence by walking through all of the Holy Doors:

- St. Peter's Basilica in Vatican City, the most famous Rome church.
- San Giovanni in Laterano (St John Lateran in Rome).
- Santa Maria Maggiore.
- Outside the Walls: Saint Paul This was Rome's largest church until St Peter's Basilica was erected. The church dedicated to the apostle Paul was built during the reign of Emperor Constantine, but was destroyed by fire in the 19th century and had to be rebuilt. Because it was built outside the city walls on the location where Paul the apostle was buried, the Rome church is known as 'Fuori le Mura.' Medallions with mosaics depicting all 265 popes can be seen around the church.

Memories

Date:

23. Baths of Caracalla

The Baths of Caracalla were created in the third century and are named after Emperor Caracalla, who, along with his father, Emperor Septimius Severus, commissioned the construction of the massive bathing complex. Together with the Colosseum, this was one of the largest structures in Roman history. The baths, which spanned 11 hectares and were lavishly decorated with exquisite mosaics, frescos, and marble cladding at the time, were Rome's largest bathing complex, accommodating over 2,500 people. The complex of cold, warm, and hot baths, pools, massage rooms, dressing rooms, receptions, and even libraries and brothels were open to the general public. Baths served a social and sporting purpose in addition to keeping people clean.

A hot-water bath was the first step in the Roman bathing regimen (calidarium). People next went to the lukewarm tepidarium and then the chilly bath (frigidarium). A swim in the natatio, an open-air pool, was frequently followed.

Memories

Date:

24. Roman sightseeing in Ostia Antica

Ostia Antica is located 30 kilometers west of Rome. This is Rome's old port city, which is now a 100-hectare archaeological park with numerous excavations. It's a great day trip from Rome. The numerous ruins can keep you occupied for hours.

The ancient port of Rome was constructed in the 7th century BCE for trade and as a military station. The harbour city did not grow greatly until the 2nd century CE. The name 'Ostia' comes from the Latin ostium, which means mouth, and refers to the city's location on the banks of the Tiber River. The nearly 100,000 people who had called this city home in its heyday began to gradually flee the city as the harbour began to silt up during the 2nd century CE.

Despite the fact that the city was frequently exploited as a source for marble, columns, and other building materials, Ostia Antica remains one of Italy's best-preserved Roman cities. If you're wondering where the sea is during your visit, be advised that it's now a few kilometers away due to shifting shore lines. The Tiber's main river has likewise shifted its route.

Memories

Date:

25. Villa d'Este & Villa Adriana

Tivoli is located 29 kilometers east of Rome. Two World Heritage-listed homes, the Renaissance Villa d'Este with a lovely interior and beautiful gardens, are located amid Tivoli's lush surrounds. The Roman excavations of Villa Adriana, Emperor Hadrian's massive villa, are well worth seeing.

If you have a longer stay in Rome, a day trip to Tivoli, which is 29 kilometers east of Rome, can be enjoyable. A variety of antique villas may be seen amid Tivoli's lush surrounds. The Villa d'Este, built in the 16th century, is a stunning Renaissance house with lovely palace gardens. Villa Adriana is a few kilometers outside of Tivoli and is the Roman ruins of Emperor Hadrian's massive villa. Palace Gregoriana is another well-known villa in Tivoli, notable for its massive waterfalls in the gardens.

Memories

Date:

Don't forget to get your FREE book below.

https://bit.ly/25PlacesParis

www.ingramcontent.com/pod-product-compliance
Lightning Source LLC
Chambersburg PA
CBHW071405080526
44587CB00017B/3181